Intimations

Selected Poems by Anna Akhmatova

T0349960

Intimations

Selected Poems by Anna Akhmatova

New and selected translations by
James E. Falen

Edited and introduction by
Kevin M. F. Platt

WHALE & STAR

CONTENTS

Anna Akhmatova
Lyricism and Endurance
Kevin M. F. Platt

It may curl like a snake in a ball,
Bewitching your heart in the still,
Or for days at a time it may call
Like a dove on a white windowsill.

Akhmatova, from "Love," 1911 (41)[1]

In the horrible years of the Yezhov Terror I spent seventeen months waiting in lines outside of Leningrad prisons. Somehow, one day I was "recognized." A blue-lipped woman standing behind me, who naturally had never heard my name before, snapped out of the stupor that was habitual for all of us and whispered into my ear (everyone spoke in a whisper there), "And can you describe this?" I answered, "I can." Then, something like a smile flashed across the place where her face had been.

Akhmatova, from "In Place of a Foreword," *Requiem*, 1957[2]

Anna Akhmatova's life and career present the unlikely story of a skilled love poet who, through no choice of her own, became a witness to mass violence, a widely recognized exemplar of endurance and moral strength, and finally a symbol of Russian national resilience. Within a few years of the publication of her first collection of poems in 1912 at the age of twenty-two, Akhmatova had been recognized by readers and by the leading literary figures of the day as an important new poetic voice. Yet her significance on the Imperial Russian cultural scene during these last chaotic and war-torn years prior to the revolutions of 1917 far exceeded the narrowly literary. In those years, Akhmatova was a cultural celebrity, who fascinated a generation not only with her poetic works but also with the personality and drama that she created around herself by means of those works. For her, poetry and personality were tied tightly together. Her most important and frequent subjects were her various roles as artist of the word, lover, muse and wife in the bohemian social scene of St. Petersburg. Akhmatova's astonishing ability to articulate her inner experience of a life at the cutting edge of modern transformations of women's identity resonated with readers, allowing them to discover vicariously the significance of the new world that was precipitously, chaotically taking shape around them.

In light of the intensely public nature of Akhmatova's poetic persona in these early years of her career, it is all the more tragic that following the Bolshevik revolution she was quickly driven into silence and obscurity. Attacked as an archaist, a representative of the dying classes of the old world and their decadent culture, by the middle 1920s she found it impossible to publish original works. In effect, she had been transformed from the lyric persona of a new generation to persona non grata of the new order. Although she would briefly reenter the public arena with collections printed in the late 1930s and in the relatively liberal publishing regime of WWII, her life in the Soviet Union until the death of Stalin in 1953 was consigned to the social margins. Living in relative poverty; scraping by publishing translations; her husband, son and friends repeatedly arrested and harassed; she herself often publicly cursed by the representatives of the state—

Akhmatova just managed to survive these darkest decades of Soviet history.

Yet even more remarkably, throughout all of these difficult years she also managed to preserve her immense dignity and unique poetic voice. At the end of her life in the late 1950s and 1960s timorous cultural bureaucrats slowly allowed her to reemerge into public life. As new generations of readers learned from retrospective collections of poetry, even if the "collective" had rejected her as an unworthy member, she herself had continued through all her years of persecution to compose poetry in which the common life of Soviet men and women, their trials and calamities, were reflected with greater truth and moral authority than any official poet could hope to attain. Having honed her poetic skills at the start of her career representing intimate experience with nuanced precision, she emerged decades later from state imposed quarantine as one of the most accurate recorders of the experience of individuals in the turbulence of Soviet history.

•

The present collection presents a broadly inclusive overview of Akhmatova's works from the earlier portion of her career, plus a more constrained selection of poems from her later years. Akhmatova's debut took place at the height of the Modernist era, Russia's Silver Age, an epoch of radical innovations in artistic form and avant-garde disdain for social conventions. Lyric poetry was once again the most prominent literary art, following a long period of eclipse by the prose fiction masterworks of the middle and late nineteenth century—the novels of Turgenev, Dostoevsky and Tolstoy. Akhmatova herself was closely associated with Modernist movements and circles through social and literary connections. Among her first public readings was an appearance in 1910 at a famous avant-garde literary salon, Viacheslav Ivanov's St. Petersburg "tower." Ivanov was one of the most influential representatives of the dominant movement of the day, Symbolism—known for its lofty oracular pretensions and tendency towards exalted aesthetic extravagance. In the following years, Akhmatova regularly appeared at the Stray Dog Café, an artistic and literary cabaret where she rubbed shoulders with diverse figures of the Modernist art scene, from the outrageous Futurist poet Vladimir Mayakovsky to the bohemian actress and dancer Olga Glebova Sudeikina, who became Akhmatova's closest friend.

Yet in the thick of flamboyant artistic experimentation, Akhmatova's poetry was striking for its altogether restrained, traditional forms. Acmeism, the poetic movement that she helped to found—together with her then husband, Nikolai Gumilev, as well as the other superlative poet of this era, Osip Mandelstam—stood in opposition to the figural excess and otherworldly pretensions of Symbolism, championing instead a lucid treatment of this-worldly human experience in strict metrical and rhyme schemes. One of the great advantages of the poems published here relates directly to this element of formal restraint—an essential feature of Akhmatova's works and literary legacy. James Falen's brilliant translations maintain a high degree of fidelity both to the sense of the original and to its chiseled classical forms, allowing one to hear the "swing" of metrical structures alien to English poetry. Readers are advised to speak these poems aloud in order to savor their acoustic texture—as generations have done with the originals in Russia, where the tradition of memorizing and reciting poetry is alive to the present day. Note that in Akhmatova's case this tradition is of special importance, given that many of her poems were preserved for decades only thanks to the memories and voices of the poet and her friends, who risked imprisonment and persecution for their association with these forbidden works.

A fine example of Falen's achievement is the "Song of the Final Meeting" (46), in which a strong stress falls on every third syllable, with some omitted syllables that seem to illustrate the lyric persona's distraught state:[3]

> The ice in my breast was unthawing,
> But my step as before remained light.
> On my left hand I found myself drawing
> The glove that was meant for the right.
>
> It appeared that the stairs were unending,
> Though I knew,—there were only three!
> In the maples a whisper of autumn
> Made a plea: "Come perish with me!
>
> I'm deceived by a fate so malicious,
> So inconstant it fills me with rue."
> And I answered: "My precious, my precious!
> So am I—and I'll die with you. . ."

Here's the song of the final meeting.
As I looked at the house in the night,
In the bedroom the candles were gleaming,
A yellow dispassionate light.

The closest American equivalents to this simplicity of language and precision of form are in the works of Emily Dickenson and Robert Frost (the latter of whom Akhmatova met late in her life).[4] Yet such comparisons cannot do justice to the Russian formal features transposed here into a new language. Ultimately, these poems are from another time and place, and Falen offers us a rare opportunity to tune in to its distant music.

Now, for all of the classicism of Akhmatova's larger formal choices, in her own self-possessed manner she was a markedly innovative poet in terms of subject matter and subtle technical inventions. In the first decades of Akhmatova's career her most frequent topic was love, yet her treatment of this timeworn concern startled contemporaries in the novelty of its intricate psychological portraiture. Although Russia had known women poets of note before, this was the first generation of women to capture center stage in Russian literary life, and Akhmatova was undoubtedly among the leaders of this revolution.[5] Casting no doubt on the universal significance of these poems (Akhmatova herself hated to be called a "poetess"), one cannot but join the poet's contemporaries in their enthrallment, for the first time, by the authentic voice of a Russian woman, articulated with unprecedented insight into her inner world.

Key innovative techniques, crucial to Akhmatova's poetic achievements and success with readers, are evident in the work reproduced above, "Song of the Final Meeting." Typically for Akhmatova's early period, this short lyric poem manages to project a far larger context of action, inviting readers to reconstruct an entire summer romance from the spare details of an autumn break-up. Short snatches of dialogue self-consciously, almost ironically enact the clichéd episodes of a love story, while suggestive details such as the heroine's confusion over her gloves and the "yellow dispassionate light" in the bedroom efficiently draw the outlines of a complex, half-concealed situation. It is in reference to these features that critics have frequently attributed to Akhmatova's poetry a novelistic quality. As Mandelstam wrote in 1922:

> Akhmatova introduced into the Russian lyric the whole of the enormous complexity and psychological richness of the nineteenth-century Russian novel. There would be no Akhmatova if there had not been Tolstoy with his *Anna Karenina*, Turgenev with his *Nest of Gentryfolk*, all of Dostoevsky and to some degree even Leskov. The genesis of Akhmatova lies entirely in Russian prose, and not in poetry. She developed her poetic form, acute and distinctive, with a backward glance at psychological prose.[6]

Mandelstam's comments notwithstanding, there is no larger "novelistic" continuity uniting the poems of Akhmatova's early collections. Yet it should also be said that a certain unity of sensibility invites the reader to imagine larger plots bringing together many of these works, or to read individual lyrics as pages torn from the intimate diary of the poet herself.[7]

One would be only half-wrong to do just that. Scholars caution against too literal an identification of the heroine of these poems with Akhmatova herself, drawing our attention to the poet's deliberate transformation of the facts of her biography into literature. Dates are changed; one identifiable face or identity merges with another; and the facts of life are recast in scenes drawn from the playbook of psychological fiction or folktale. Yet to draw an absolute distinction between the poet's life and art would also fail to capture the essence of the early Akhmatova. In those last years of the Russian Empire she was a rising star, a celebrity of avant-garde society, whose marriages, romances and liaisons were a matter of curiosity and speculation. Akhmatova was endlessly photographed and represented in works of art and "as for the poems dedicated to her, they'd make more volumes than her own collected works," as Joseph Brodsky noted.[8] The poet flourished in the limelight, intentionally teasing the public with tantalizing, suggestive episodes and details. Undoubtedly, Akhmatova's poems have the exaggerated character of a dramatic gesture or a striking posture. Yet this larger-than-life quality was just as surely a key feature of her physical presence and comportment. For her, life was as much a part of her poetry as poetry was a part of her life. As Andrew Wachtel has recently observed, in this linkage of public and private, of reality and invention, Akhmatova realized the Modernist ambition of merging life and art.[9]

This intertwining of lived experience with poetic representation was to persist in Akhmatova's works to the end of her life. Yet as the stakes of a literary life changed, so too did the stakes of representing it. In her early years her role as femme fatale, both on the social scene and in poetic refraction, had a good deal of the theatrical about it. In her later years history itself assigned Akhmatova the role of "woman in confrontation with fate." The tragic, unplanned transformation of her dramatic pose into a reality became fully apparent only in poems of the 1930s such as "Sentence" (125). This work is part of a celebrated larger cycle of poems, *Requiem*, in which Akhmatova's own ordeals in connection with the imprisonment of her son, husband and friends have been rendered into an expression of the experience of all Russian women in the Stalinist Great Terror. As the second epigraph above, taken from *Requiem*, lucidly demonstrates, by this time Akhmatova was no longer a unique symbol of modern life. Rather, she had become an everywoman speaking for the many others like her who had no voice of their own. In her early years many already concurred with Mandelstam's remark of 1916 that Akhmatova's poetry was "already close to becoming a symbol of Russian greatness." By the end of her career her significance as a living monument to the endurance of pre-revolutionary Russian culture and values had become proverbial. Metaphor had become reality.

•

Anna Akhmatova was born Anna Gorenko on June 23, 1889 in Bolshoi Fontan in Ukraine, then a part of the

Russian Empire.[10] Her father Andrey Antonovich Gorenko was a Ukrainian naval officer and her mother Inna Erazmovna (née Stogova) was a Russian from the Novgorod region. Both were members of the lesser nobility who held decidedly progressive political views—Gorenko, his wife and both of his sisters are known to have had associations with the terrorist organization The People's Will, responsible for the assassination of Tsar Alexander II in 1881. Yet according to the peculiar logic of Russian society during the late Imperial era, ties to radical revolutionaries were not incompatible with bourgeois lifestyles and appointments in establishment institutions. Gorenko had earlier in his career been an instructor at the Naval Academy in Petersburg, but was relieved of this position under suspicion of illegal political activity. Subsequently, he had been reinstated and assigned to service in the Black Sea Fleet. However, by the time of Anna's birth he had resigned his commission at the rank of captain and was working as a writer for a newspaper in Odessa. He was later to publish a novella and some short stories, and was active in commerce groups and philosophical societies. Shortly after the birth of Anna, in 1890, he moved his family to St. Petersburg's most fashionable suburb, Tsarskoe Selo, the summer residence of the tsars. Akhmatova's girlhood was passed in this upper-crust setting—an exclusive school, French lessons, proper behavior, concerts, etc. Her memoirs record that she learned to read from the alphabet book written by Tolstoy and first heard Russian poetry from her mother, who read her the works of Nikolai

Nekrasov.[11] Both the stately scene of allées, fountains and statues in Tsarskoe Selo's manicured parks and the Black Sea shore in Ukraine, where the family returned in the summers, were to leave their mark in her poetry.

When she was fifteen, Akhmatova's parents separated and her mother moved with Akhmatova and her siblings to Evpatoria in Ukraine, leaving her father in St. Petersburg. She finished preparatory school and began university studies in Ukraine's capital Kiev, but was by this time already being drawn into literary bohemia. The young poet Nikolai Gumilev, whom she knew from Tsarskoe Selo, began pursuing her in 1906 and courted her intermittently up to their marriage in 1910. He also became the first to publish Akhmatova's poems in 1907, in his short-lived journal *Sirius*. Gumilev was a questing spirit whose first collections (1905 and 1908) were strongly influenced by the mystical strivings of Symbolism. He took frequent trips to Africa to hunt big game, studied French literature in Paris, traveled extensively in Italy and generally labored to wrap himself in an aura of romantic exoticism. Immediately after their marriage, the young couple took a trip to Paris, where Akhmatova met the young Amedeo Modigliani who took her wandering in the streets of the French capital and left a striking sketch of the young poet in her own possession. Upon their return to Russia, Gumilev and Akhmatova settled in Tsarskoe Selo, in rooms decorated with Gumilev's African trophies, and for the next few years became fixtures in the St. Petersburg cultural scene—she, perhaps, more than he, since his presence was punctuated by continuing extended trips to Africa. Summers were spent on Gumilev's mother's country estate Slepnevo, in the Tver district. In 1912 Akhmatova gave birth to their son Lev Gumilev, whose early infancy and childhood were spent in the care of his grandmother, Gumilev's mother. By all accounts, the marriage of the two poets was shaky and often strained. Neither was much interested in leading a conventional life and both were inclined to romantic attachments, flirtations and liaisons. Gumilev's frequent travel turned into a more or less permanent absence in 1914, when he quickly enlisted following the outbreak of the First World War.

During the few years between her debut and the onset of the war Akhmatova had matured into a major literary figure. In order to appease her father's wish that she not bring shame on the family name, she had adopted the name "Akhmatova" with her first publications. It is derived from the name of a distant maternal forbear, descendant of an even more distant Tatar prince, Akhmat Khan. Brodsky quips that her name, with its "five open a's […] was her first successful line," and although he also remarks that "she didn't mean to be exotic," it seems likely that the choice was in part a reflection of the Modernist fascination with the myth of the Orient.[12] Following her first appearances and the publication of her first collection, *Evening*, in 1912, Akhmatova quickly won over both the literary world and a devoted readership. In revolt against the tutelage and methods of Symbolism, she and Gumilev, Mandelstam, Sergei Gorodetskii, and others founded first the group "The Poet's Guild" in 1911 and then their own "movement," Acmeism—although typically for this age of proliferating "isms," the Acmeists never numbered more than a handful. Their school of writing, influenced by the French Parnassian movement's emphasis on perfection of form, was dedicated to treatment of concrete subjects in precise, finely honed language.

Although Gumilev published several programmatic works, it was the poetry of Mandelstam and Akhmatova that gave the group its identity and that has endured among the emblematic literary accomplishments of the Silver Age. The culmination of this period of productivity and public acclaim was Akhmatova's second collection, *Rosary*, which appeared in the first months of 1914. Almost without exception, Akhmatova's attention in this collection remained focused on the topic of love. Yet as the book's title suggests, Akhmatova's work frequently began to incorporate religious motifs, not in the form of abstract meditation on religious or philosophical themes (this was more Mandelstam's territory), but rather in the form of a simple, almost reflexive Orthodox religious sentiment.

By early 1917, Russia's disastrous prosecution of the war had completely discredited the tsarist regime, leading to Nicholas II's abdication and ceding of power to a provisional government. Half a year of political infighting and civil unrest ended in the Bolshevik seizure of power in the October Revolution. The following years of civil war and then consolidation of Soviet power transformed the social fabric of Russia, and along with it Akhmatova's literary and personal milieu. By the time of the Revolution, Akhmatova's relationship with Gumilev had utterly collapsed. When in 1918 he returned to Petrograd (as St. Petersburg had been renamed during the war in a fit of anti-German sentiment) after spending six months in Paris in another woman's arms, Akhmatova demanded and received a divorce. At this time, Akhmatova worked as a librarian and lived for several years with the assyriologist and minor poet Vladimir Shileiko, whom she unofficially married. Yet this arrangement lasted only until 1921, when Akhmatova left Shileiko to move in with friends. The literary world of St. Petersburg in those years centered on state-sponsored projects and institutions, such as the House of Literature and the House of Arts. It was a hungry time of cultural ferment, in which many imagined that a new world was being born. Yet the birth was by no means a painless one: the bohemian amusements of pre-revolutionary cultural life had given way to a life of deadly seriousness. In 1921 Gumilev, with whom Akhmatova still had significant social contact, was arrested and shot for his alleged involvement in a counterrevolutionary plot.

Akhmatova published three partially overlapping collections of poetry during the war and the immediate post-revolutionary years: *White Flock* (1917), *Plantain* (1920) and *MCMXXI* (1921). Civic notes sounded in all of these collections—take, for example, the patriotic poems "Prayer" (80) of 1915 and "When people pondered suicide..." (96) of 1917 or the meditation on social turmoil "Why is this age more bleak..." (101). Yet it should also be said that, considering what

Akhmatova and her country as a whole were undergoing, the poet's reluctance to engage history or politics in any straightforward manner is remarkable. Consider, for instance, this poem of 1917:

> That voice, disputing with the silent scene,
> Has conquered silence—and it reigns no more.
> It's still inside me—like a song or grief—
> That final winter that preceded war.
>
> More white than the Basilica of Smolny,
> More strange than Summer Garden and more fair
> It was. We never knew that soon we'd only
> Look backward in complete despair. (78)

For all the poet's attention here to the momentous events of national history, and for all the growth of her poetic system to encompass civic experience in common public spaces (the geography she describes here is that of central St. Petersburg), she remains faithful to her own voice and themes. Typically for her writing of these years, history's movement is visible primarily through the traces it leaves on the intimate life and relationships of the poetic persona. Constant in her creative impulses, Akhmatova never wrote "war poems," nor did she write "poetry of revolution," either for it or against.

For champions of the new revolutionary order, this fidelity in style and purpose was clear evidence of Akhmatova's cultural superannuation. In 1921, the critic and author Kornei Chukovsky delivered a lecture in the House of Literature, subsequently published as an article, comparing Akhmatova and the futurist poet

Mayakovsky as representatives of the literary past and future, and calling Akhmatova "the last poet of Orthodoxy" and the "heiress of all that is most valuable in the richness of pre-revolutionary culture."[13] Chukovsky, with whom Akhmatova was on friendly terms, concluded his article with a call for a cultural convergence that could make a place in Soviet Russia for both the Mayakovskys and the Akhmatovas. Others who shared Chukovsky's assessment of Akhmatova were not so inclined towards a path of reconciliation. Mayakovsky himself publicly denounced her in these years as an anachronism who should be purged from Soviet literature. The most culturally alert Bolshevik leader, Leon Trotsky, identified her as a relic of Russia's past and mocked her religious sentiment in his influential tract *Literature and Revolution*. The positions of these leading figures were echoed by countless revolutionary foot-soldiers: "Everyone is aware that A. Akhmatova is a mystic, a nun, reactionary in her ideology and therefore disposed to be our adversary."[14] Critically besieged, by the middle of the 1920s Akhmatova had been effectively squeezed out of the press—her last publication of original poetry before what was to be a long period of public silence was a selection of poems in a 1925 anthology. In the late 1920s and 1930s, although still attempting without success to convince the authorities to allow publication of her collected works, she turned to literary translation and critical articles, especially regarding Russia's national poet Alexander Pushkin. During the late 1920s she became close to the art critic Nikolai Punin, with whom she lived from 1926 until the late 1930s in a small apartment together with Punin's wife Anna Arens, their daughter and Akhmatova's son Lev Gumilev.

In retrospect, it was perhaps a stroke of good fortune that Akhmatova's public presence as a poet dwindled out so quickly in the post-revolutionary era. During the 1920s, Soviet cultural life was engulfed in clashes between the members of an unruly throng of associations and movements—proletarian, avant-garde, constructivist, etc. The Bolshevik leadership, limited in resources, preoccupied with military and political consolidation and lacking a party line on culture, generally refrained from interfering in literary affairs. Politically engaged criticism was by no means reticent in raising the revolutionary standard in attacking 'representatives of the bourgeois and decadent art of the past,' such as Akhmatova. In general, however, this was a relatively vegetarian era. In the cacophony of competition among groups vying to occupy the position of "true" voice of the revolution, the silencing of Akhmatova was not the result of any organized campaign of repression, nor did it take the form of police action against her. Such campaigns would come into fashion only later. At the end of the 1920s and the beginning of the 1930s, as Joseph Stalin exerted his tyrannical authority over Soviet society, the state imposed a new system of bureaucratized cultural life in service to state-formulated goals. In the often brutal implementation of this new order, authors branded as non-conformists and 'class-enemies' were hounded into submission or forced into emigration. As the 1930s wore on, they were subject to arrest, imprisonment and murder at the hands of the secret police. While Akhmatova herself was not the target of such measures, they struck with regularity on all sides of her: Punin and Lev Gumilev were arrested, released and rearrested during the middle 1930s; Mandelstam, with whom Akhmatova still shared a deep friendship, was arrested, exiled, then arrested again in the late 1930s. His death in a transit camp reflected the fate of many of Russia's intellectuals and literary figures during the Great Terror of 1937-1938. That Akhmatova herself did not share this fate is perhaps thanks only to her cultural "invisibility" during these years. Her monument to the survivors and victims of this paroxysm of state-sponsored violence was the cycle of poems *Requiem*, which was to remain unpublished, preserved in the memory of Akhmatova and her circle until many decades later.

In works of Akhmatova's later career one is once again struck by her constancy of style—the laconic, precise turns of phrase; characteristic sparseness of figural language; and stockpile of familiar vocabulary and images drawn from folk poetry and religious culture. One recognizes, too, her meticulous accounts of human relationships and psychology. Yet her maturation is also impossible to miss. From her poetic origins in intensely lyrical intimate experience, Akhmatova steadily progressed towards the horizon of archetypal, universal significance. Consider her vision of Cleopatra's last days:

She's kissed the dead lips of her Antony's corpse,
Has shed on her knees before Caesar hot tears. . .
Her servants have fled. The victorious horns
Of Rome are resounding, and darkness appears.

And in came the last whom her beauty enslaved,
Most stately and tall, and he blushed as he swore:
   "He'll send you before him in triumph, a slave."
But calm as a swan's was her neck as before.

Tomorrow they'll shackle her children in chains.
So little to do. . . but to jest with this man. . .
And then the black snake, as a parting to pain,
To place on her breast with dispassionate hand. (127)

In these lines of 1940, Akhmatova refracts her familiar early subject, romantic love, through the prism of history to create a portrait of the human will confronting an ineluctable fate. Akhmatova herself had been transformed by this time into an iconic figure of national resilience and human wisdom. Whereas at the start of her career she had played the standard roles of the Silver Age to perfection, by the end she had become a unique cultural authority, lone guardian of cultural continuity, and inspiring example of survival, grace and sheer grit.

The immediate aftermath of the Great Terror of the 1930s brought a partial liberalization of Russian public life, and for the first time since the mid-1920s Akhmatova was able to publish a heavily censored, slim volume of poems in 1940. Yet in a typical signal of the ambivalence of the authorities towards the poet, the book was withdrawn from sale and circulation later that same year. However, the outbreak of the Second World War in the summer of 1941 initiated processes of liberalization in the public sphere once again. The demands of mass mobilization led to significant departures from ideological orthodoxy, including a partial rehabilitation of Russian religious institutions and expressions of national pride. Soviet men and women rose to the defense of their state and society, and Akhmatova was no exception. She spent the war in evacuation in Central Asia, publishing patriotic poems such as "Courage" (131), as well as a volume of *Selected Poems* in 1943 in Tashkent. By the end of the war, when she returned to Leningrad to take up residence with her son who had been allowed to return from exile, Akhmatova had gained a position of prominence in Soviet cultural life such as she had never before enjoyed. Yet it was not to last. Party elites, concerned lest the liberal regime of the war years loosen their grip on power, unleashed a new wave of repressive interventions into Soviet culture. Akhmatova and the short story writer Mikhail Zoshchenko became the target of a landmark Central Committee resolution that labeled them as class enemies. Andrei Zhdanov, the Party's ideology watchdog, extended the attack at a meeting of Leningrad writers where he labeled Akhmatova a "half-whore and half-nun who mixes fornication with prayer."[15] In the following months she was expelled from the Soviet Writers' Union and subjected to vicious attacks in the press. Two years later, in 1949, her son was arrested once again, as was Punin, who died of illness in the camps. Akhmatova, in despair, composed poems in praise of Stalin, which were published in a leading Soviet journal in 1950, yet nevertheless failed to secure the release of her son.

That event was to come only after the death of the dictator himself in 1953. By 1956, his successor as Soviet leader Nikita Khrushchev had initiated broad-ranging processes of liberalization, repudiating much of the legacy of the Stalinist years. Lev Gumilev was among many political prisoners who returned to Soviet society from the camps. Although the "thaw" of Soviet society in this era was a slow process of negotiation afflicted by many reversals and false starts, the general result for Akhmatova was that she could finally, in this last decade of her life, pursue her craft without fear of state persecution. She published critical works and retrospective volumes of her poetry in which Soviet readers could finally learn that she had continued to write through the decades of state-imposed silence— chronicling the experience of men and women in the grip of the Soviet social experiment, projecting that life against mythological, biblical and classical archetypes. In these years Akhmatova completed her monumental epic work *A Poem Without a Hero*, dedicated to the cultural and social history of Silver Age Russia. Although her late publications were still subject to censorship, the censor had a far lighter hand in these years than in previous decades. A circle of young, non-conformist poets took shape around her, including the young Joseph Brodsky. Foreign visitors such as Robert Frost were allowed to make contact with Akhmatova, and she herself traveled outside of the Soviet Union for the first time since its formation to receive a prestigious literary prize in Italy from the Community of European Writers in 1964. In 1965 she traveled to Oxford, where she received an honorary degree. At her death, in 1966, she was publicly mourned inside of Russia and outside as one of the greatest poets of the twentieth century, who witnessed and memorialized both the great hopes and the great catastrophes of her era.

Suggestions for Further Reading

Other editions of Akhmatova's work in English:

Anna Akhmatova. *The Complete Poems of Anna Akhmatova*. Judith Hemschemeyer, trans. Roberta Reeder, ed. Somerville, Mass.: Zephyr Press, 2000.

Anna Akhmatova. *Poems*. D. M. Thomas, trans. New York: Knopf, 2006.

Anna Akhmatova. *The Word that Causes Death's Defeat: Poems of Memory*. Nancy K. Anderson, ed. and trans. New Haven, Conn.: Yale University Press, 2004.

Anna Akhmatova. *My Half Century: Selected Prose*. Ronald Meyer, ed. Ann Arbor, Mich.: Ardis, 1992.

Anna Akhmatova. *Poems*. Lyn Coffin, trans. New York: W. W. Norton, 1983.

Anna Akhmatova. *Poems*. Stanley Kunitz and Max Hayward., trans. New York: Knopf, 2006.

Memoirs and Biography:

Roberta Reeder. *Anna Akhmatova: Poet and Prophet*. New York: Saint Martin's Press, 1994.

Lydia Chukovskaya. *The Akhmatova Journals*. Milena Michalski, Sylva Rubashova and Peter Norman, trans. New York: Farrar, Straus & Giroux, 1994.

Konstantin Polivanov, ed. *Anna Akhmatova and Her Circle*. Patricia Beriozkina, trans. Fayetteville, Ark.: University of Arkansas Press, 1993.

Scholarly Studies of Akhmatova:

Susan Amert. *In a Shattered Mirror: the Later Poetry of Anna Akhmatova.* Stanford, Cal.: Stanford University Press, 1992.

Amanda Haight. Anna Akhmatova: *A Poetic Pilgrimage.* New York: Oxford University Press, 1976.

Translator's Note and Acknowledgments
James E. Falen

These translations of verse by the Russian poet Anna Akhmatova (1889-1966) draw most heavily on the poet's early work, poems that she wrote before the Revolutions of 1917 and in the decade that followed. Her first book of verse, *Evening* (published in 1912), brought her considerable acclaim and a wide readership, both of which her subsequent collections confirmed. By the mid-twenties, however, the repressive nature of Soviet reality made the fate of poets, as of everyone else, precarious. Subjected to severe official criticism as a hostile relic of the bourgeois past and as irrelevant to the new Soviet era, Akhmatova, for some two decades, fell into an enforced silence. Except for translations and a few poems that were published during the second world war, little of her work appeared in print. By the end of the war she was under renewed attack and, after her expulsion from the Soviet Writers' Union in 1946, was once again denied publication. Late in her life, in the post-Stalin era, Akhmatova's stature as a major twentieth-century poet was widely acknowledged, and her work at last began to reappear in print.

With regard to the form of her verse, Akhmatova is not a modernist poet—not at least in her shorter lyrics, to which I have limited myself in this selection. She wrote few poems in free verse and adheres for the most part to the meter and rhyme of the Russian classical tradition; although she has a particular fondness for the ternary meters (anapests, dactyls, and amphibrachs). Pushkin and other major poets of the early nineteenth century generally favored iambic and, to a lesser degree, trochaic meters for their lyrical verse, which became the canonical forms of Russian classical poetry. Only Lermontov, notably, found the ternary meters especially congenial. Gradually, over the course of the nineteenth century, other poets experimented with these meters, finding them particularly appropriate for the Russian language with its many polysyllabic, single-stressed words. In the twentieth century both Pasternak and Akhmatova have used the ternary meters extensively in their effort to reinvigorate the language of poetry.

Akhmatova's varied use of such rhythms tends to round or soften the contours of her tightly-structured forms, to lend an almost conversational familiarity to the tone of her voice. Often, as well, she will begin a poem with the word "And" or some other conjunctive, which gives the listener a sense that he has entered the poem after it has already begun, perhaps as a sort of interior monologue that becomes audible to the listener/reader only in mid stream. Many of her love poems are like private letters that reveal an emotional or psychological crisis; and the reader has a sense that he or she, if not being addressed directly, is overhearing a private communication to a current or former or imagined lover. The word "You," invoking her addressee or interlocutor, is particularly prominent in such poems. Akhmatova's early poetry is especially powerful in these expressions of intimacy; in the psychological tensions she conveys; and in the precision and clarity of her voice, the voice of a woman sounding a new note in Russian literature.

In the final section of this small anthology, under the rubric "Other Poems," I have included several lyrics from Akhmatova's "silent" years and from the last decade of her life, when the love-laden lyrics of her youth gave way to the claims of memory and time, to the grief she felt for the suffering of her friends and countrymen, and to reflections on the power and fate of poetry. I have sought in these translations to approximate both the sense and the sensibility of Akhmatova's verse, to give some semblance of both its form and its spirit, as I heard them in these poems.

I should note that in the Russian originals many of the poems bear no titles. Where this is the case, I have followed the custom of using the first line (or a part of the first line) as such.

I would like to take this opportunity to express my gratitude to Kevin M. F. Platt for the introduction and the notes he has contributed to this volume and to thank him for the keen critical eye with which he read my work in draft. His perceptive comments have encouraged me to rethink and rework a number of lines in these English versions of Akhmatova's poetry. He is not, of course, responsible for the inadequacies that remain.

Finally, both Mr. Platt and I offer many thanks to Enrique Martínez Celaya for his support and commitment to this project, as well as to Catherine Wallack and the rest of the staff at the Whale & Star publishing house for their excellent work producing this volume.

From *Evening*

LOVE

It may curl like a snake in a ball,
Bewitching your heart in the still,
Or for days at a time it may call
Like a dove on a white windowsill.

It flashes in dazzles of frost
And drowses in willowy trees,
But leads without fail to the loss
Of happiness, freedom, and peace.

It elicits a sobbing so sweet,
Like the prayer of a sorrowful viol,
And how dreadful it is when it's seen
In a still unfamiliar smile.

24 November 1911
Tsarskoye Selo

IN TSARSKOYE SELO[16]

I

They're leading the horses along the allée,
How wavy their long curried manes.
O City of riddles, enchanting and gay,
I'm sad that I loved you in pain. . .

How strange to recall the soul's yearning,
Its panting in death-fevered rue,
When now I'm so playful and merry,
I sing like my pink cockatoo.

No omen of pain in my breast;
If you wish, in my eyes you may gaze.
I dislike just the time before sunset,
The wind, and the words: "Go away."

22 February 1911
Tsarskoye Selo

II

. . . And there my marble double stays,
Laid low beneath a maple tree,
He gave the rippling lake his face
And listens to the rustling green.

And there the glinting raindrops clean
The crusted edges of his wound. . .
But wait, my cold and white-washed dream,
I too shall turn to marble soon.

1911

III

A swarthy youth once walked these lanes[17]
And by these lakeshore paths he yearned;
A hundred years have we sustained
Those rustling footsteps, faintly heard.

Low stumps are covered with a mat
Of prickly needles, pines and firs. . .
Here lay his cocked, three-cornered hat
And tattered tome of Parny's verse.

24 September 1911
Tsarskoye Selo

MEMORY OF SUNLIGHT DIMS IN MY HEART

Memory of sunlight dims in my heart.
Yellowing grass,
Wind and the snowflakes drifting apart. . .
Slowly they pass.

Water in narrow canals going still—
Ice in its pen.
Nothing can happen and now never will,
Never again!

Willowtree spreading its fan in a sky
Emptied of light.
Maybe it's better in fact that I
Wasn't your wife.

Memory of sunlight dims in the heart.
Is it the Dark?
Maybe it is! . . The winter can start
Overnight.

30 January 1911
Kiev

SONG OF THE FINAL MEETING

The ice in my breast was unthawing,
But my step as before remained light.
On my left hand I found myself drawing
The glove that was meant for the right.

It appeared that the stairs were unending,
Though I knew,—there were only three!
In the maples a whisper of autumn
Made a plea: "Come perish with me!

I'm deceived by a fate so malicious,
So inconstant it fills me with rue."
And I answered: "My precious, my precious!
So am I—and I'll die with you. . ."

Here's the song of the final meeting.
As I looked at the house in the night,
In the bedroom the candles were gleaming,
A yellow dispassionate light.

29 September 1911
Tsarskoye Selo

HEART TO HEART IS NEVER CHAINED

Heart to heart is never chained,
If you want to—leave.
Greater happiness awaits
Those whose paths are free.

I don't weep or make complaint,
Happiness is not my curse,
Do not kiss me, I am faint,—
Death will kiss me first.

Days of biting languor blew
With the winter snows.
Why, oh why, should I find you
Better than the one I chose?

Spring 1911

ON A WHITE NIGHT[18]

Ah no, I didn't lock the door,
The candles stayed unlit,
You'll never know, though all worn out,
I wouldn't sleep a bit.

To watch the jagged streaks of firs
At sunset fade from view,
Enraptured by a voice I heard
That sounded so like you.

And then to know that all is lost,
That life is cursèd spite!
Oh, I was so completely sure
That you'd come back that night.

6 February 1911
Tsarskoye Selo

TO THE MUSE

My sister-the-Muse took a glance at my face,
A glance that was crystal and bright,
And took from my finger the tiny gold band,
My first vernal gift and delight.

O Muse! you can see, how happy they are—
The widows, the wives, and the maids. . .
Oh, better to die on the scaffold by far,
Than ever to suffer these chains.

I know, as I chant, that I'm fated to tear
The delicate daisy to shreds,
For here on this earth every soul has to bear
The torment of love and the dread.

A candle I burn till the dawn and the dew
And no one at all do I miss.
But no, I refuse, I refuse, I refuse
To know how another is kissed.

Tomorrow my mirror, with laughter, will say:
"Your gaze isn't crystal or bright. . ."
And softly I'll answer: "The Muse took away
God's gift in the night."

10 October 1911
Tsarskoye Selo

49

THE GRAY-EYED KING

Hosanna to you, inescapable pain!
Our fair, gray-eyed king was just yesterday slain.

The still, autumn evening was sultry and red;
My husband, returning, was calm when he said:

"They brought him, you know, from the hunt into town;
His body beside an old oak tree was found.

The queen's to be pitied. So young and so gay!..
Her hair overnight has gone totally gray."

He took up his pipe from the mantel and then
Went off to his work for the night once again.

And now I'll awaken my daughter so fair,
And into her lovely gray eyes I will stare.

Beyond the dark window the willow trees sound:
"No more on this earth is your king to be found."

11 December 1910
Tsarskoye Selo

SO I LIVE LIKE A BIRD

So I live like a bird in a clock,
I don't envy those birds in a flock.
Wind me up and I crow—
But I'd like you to know:
Only someone I hate
Would I wish such a fate.

1911

From *Rosary*

IN THE EVENING

The music in the garden rang—
Like grief—ineffably precise;
From oysters on a bed of ice
There came the seaside's pungent tang.

He told me: "I'm a faithful friend!"
And then he lightly touched my dress.
But how unlike a warm caress
I found the contact of those hands.

One strokes a cat or bird that way;
One looks at graceful riders so.
There's laughter in his eyes of gray
Beneath their golden lashes' glow.

And mournful violins sing out
Behind the smoke that's drifting past;
"Thank heaven that it's come about:
Your love and you, alone at last."

1913

WE'RE ALL REVELERS HERE[19]

We're all revelers here, and harlots,
How unhappy we are in this crowd!
On the walls the birds and flowers
Are dreaming of far-away clouds.

You're smoking an ebony pipe,
And the air is so strangely dim;
I'm wearing a skirt that's tight,
To make myself even more slim.

The windows are boarded forever.
Outside—is it frosty or wet?
Your eyes have a look that resembles
The eyes of a vigilant cat.

Oh, my heart is so filled with anguish!
Am I waiting to hear death's knell?
But that woman dancing the tango
Will certainly soon be in hell.

1 January 1913

HOW OFTEN, AFTER WIND AND FROST

How often, after wind and frost,
Before the hearth I loved to rest.
But there I failed to guard my heart,
And someone stole it from my breast.

The New Year's Day goes grandly by,
The roses' stems are moist as dew,
And in this breast I cannot find
The trembling dragonflies I knew.

It wasn't hard to guess the thief,
I knew him by his eyes, you see.
How dreadful, though, that soon enough
He'll give his booty back to me.

January 1914

TRUE TENDERNESS CAN'T BE MISTAKEN

True tenderness can't be mistaken
For anything else, and it purrs.
In vain do you wrap so sedately
My shoulders and breast in these furs.
And in vain are these words submissive
You murmur of love without end;
Oh, I know so well these persistent
Importunate glances you send!

December 1913
Tsarskoye Selo

THERE'S A SMILE THAT I GIVE TO A FEW

There's a smile that I give to a few,
Where my lips, as you see, barely lift;
But I'm keeping it now just for you—
After all, it was love's precious gift.
Never mind that you're wicked and bold,
Never mind that you love others, too.
Up ahead is a pulpit of gold,
And beside me my charcoal-eyed groom.

1913

WE MET THAT DAY ONE FINAL TIME

We met that day one final time,
As always, by the river pier.
The Neva's waters then were high,
And in the town a flood was feared.[20]

He spoke of summer and about
A woman-poet as a joke.
How well I know the royal house,
Paul's fortress, and the dungeon's yoke!

The very air was not our own,
but wondrous—like a gift from God.
And in that moment I was shown
The last of all my frenzied songs.

January 1914

DO NOT CRUMPLE, MY DEAREST, MY LETTER

Do not crumple, my dearest, my letter.
Read it all, read it through to the end.
I no longer can be the fair stranger,
Passerby on your path, my friend.

Do not glower or frown in a temper.
Your belovèd am I, the one.
Not a shepherdess, no, nor a princess,
And I haven't for years been a nun—

In this gray, in this everyday dress,
In these shoes with the downtrodden heels. . .
But I still have a burning embrace
And these eyes still enormous with fears.

Do not crumple, my dearest, my letter,
Don't weep at an intimate lie,
But deep in your tattered old satchel
Keep my letter uncrumpled and dry.

1912
Tsarskoye Selo

VERSES ABOUT PETERSBURG

I

Once more Saint Isaac's lofty head
Is draped in silver strands,
While frozen in impatient dread
Great Peter's steed still stands.

From blackened flues the sultry winds
Sweep cinders near and far. . .
Ah! How his city with its sins
Dissatisfies the Czar.

II

Calm and even beats my heart,
What care I if years may pass!
Underneath Galérny Arch
Our two shadows still shall last.

Through my eyelids, almost closed,
I can scc you hcrc with me,
In your hand you always hold
My unopened fan, I see.

Since we stood here side by side
In that blessèd wondrous time,
When the Summer Garden sky
Saw the rosy moon arise,—

I no longer need to wait
By some hateful window blind,
I don't need to meet in pain—
All my love is satisfied.

You are free, and I am free,
Better days will soon begin—
By the Neva's shadowed waters,
Where, above us, never falters
Emperor Peter's frigid grin.[21]

1913

ONCE I CAME TO SEE THE POET
to Alexander Blok [22]

Once I came to see the poet.
Noon it was, precisely. Sunday.
Quiet in the spacious room,
And outside the windows—frost

And a raspberry sun
In the shaggy bluish smoke. . .
And my silent host
Peering keenly at me!

He has eyes that one
Must remember always,
I had better watch myself
And not even glance at them.

But I will. . . recall the conversation,
And the smoky noon, that Sunday
In the tall, gray house
By the Neva's sea gates.

January 1914

WILL YOU FORGIVE ME THESE
NOVEMBER DAYS

Will you forgive me these November days?
The Neva's canals and their trembling blaze.
These scant decorations of tragical autumn.

November 1913
St. Petersburg

I DO NOT WANT YOUR LOVE, MY FRIEND

I do not want your love, my friend—
It's safer where it now resides. . .
Believe me, I will never send
Impassioned letters to your bride.
But take some wise advice from me,
And let her read the verse I wrote,
My portraits you should let her keep—
For this is how good grooms must dote!
And foolish women always need
The sense of total victory gained,
Far more than friendship's glowing creed
Or relics of once tender days. . .
When with your charming girl you've spent
Your pennysworth of happiness,
And when your sated soul is rent,
Repelled and riven with distress,
To my triumphant night again
Do not apply. You've no allure.
And how could I assist you then?
For happiness I am no cure.

1914

From *White Flock*

THE ROAD BY THE SEASIDE GOES DIM

The road by the seaside goes dim,
The lanterns are yellow and bright.
I'm calm in my soul, but of him
You shouldn't be talking tonight.
You're charming, and we'll become friends. . .
We'll wander, and kiss, and grow old. . .
And moons will proceed overhead,
Like stars made of snow, in the cold.

1914

SONG ABOUT A SONG

Like freezing winds at first
It comes to burn and sear,
But then inside it bursts
In one great salty tear.

And then the evil breast
Is filled with rue, and sad.
But it will not forget
This tender grief it had.

I sow, but others come
To gather fruit. Indeed!
Please bless, O Lord above,
The buoyant band that reaps!

And now, in thanks to you,
Let me be bold enough
To give the world I knew
A thing more pure than love.

1916
Slepnyovo

YES, HE WAS JEALOUS

Yes, he was jealous, and worried and tender,
And loved me like sunlight that comes from the Lord,
And only to silence the songs it remembered,
He killed the white bird I'd always adored.

He entered my chamber at sunset and said:
"Oh, love me and laugh, write verse and be free!"
I buried the bird and the songs that were dead
Behind the round well by the old alder tree.

I gave him my promise that I wouldn't cry.
But deep in my breast my heart turned to stone,
And now it just seems. . . wherever I fly,
I'll hear the sweet voice of the bird I once owned.

Fall 1914

THE LACQUER OF BLUE IN THE SKY
GREW GRAY

The lacquer of blue in the sky grew gray
And the ocarina's song more plain.
It's only a pipe made of clay,
It hasn't a cause for such complaint?
Who told it the tale of my sins,
And why is it setting me free? . .
Or is it a voice repeating
Your latest songs to me?

1912

IT WAS A COOL, COOL DAY THAT DAY

It was a cool, cool day that day
In Peter's wonder-ridden town.
A crimson blaze the sunset lay,
As slowly shadows gathered round.

Oh, let him spurn these eyes of mine,
My faithful and prophetic gift;
A life of verses he will find,
The prayer of my disdainful lips.

Winter 1913

THERE IS IN HUMAN CLOSENESS A DIVIDE
To N.V.N.[23]

There is in human closeness a divide
That even love and passion cross in vain;
Let lips in dreadful silence be entwined,
And still the loving heart will break in twain.

And friendship, too, is powerless, you see,
And so are years of joy and sacred fire,
For then the soul was innocent and free
From langourously sensual desire.

Oh, all who strive to cross this line are mad,
And those who do so—only anguish meet. . .
And now you know the reason I am sad,
That underneath your hand my heart won't beat.

1915

A REPLY
To V.A. Komarovsky [24]

What strange, unfathomed words arrived
To chill this silent April eve.
You knew that in my soul still thrived
The dreadful news of Passion Week.

I hadn't heard those tolling bells
That floated in the utter blue.
For seven days bronze laughter swelled,
And silver lamentations flew.

While I, with covered eyes and face,
As if before eternal parting,
Was motionless and lay in wait
Of some still nameless, dreaded heartache.

Spring 1914
Tsarskoye Selo

PARTING

A dusky sloping pathway
Runs darkly up ahead.
Just yesterday, impassioned,
He begged me: "Don't forget."
And now are only breezes
And shepherds calling out
And agitated cedars
Beside a freshet's fount.

Spring 1914
St. Petersburg

I DON'T THINK OF YOU FONDLY OR OFTEN

I don't think of you fondly or often,
And your life isn't much to my taste;
But the mark of our casual meeting
Hasn't yet from my soul been effaced.

I ignore your red house on purpose,
Your red house on the brown river shore;
But I know that I bitterly bother
All that sun-dappled peace you adore.

And though *you* weren't the one who came calling,
Seeking love from my lips in the night,
Nor the one who in golden-hued verses
Made my longings immortal and bright—

Still I cast secret spells on the future,
When the evenings are totally blue,
And I sense in the distance a meeting,
An unshunnable meeting with you.

1913

THAT VOICE, DISPUTING WITH THE SILENT SCENE

That voice, disputing with the silent scene,
Has conquered silence—and it reigns no more.
It's still inside me—like a song or grief—
That final winter that preceded war.

More white than the Basilica of Smolny,
More strange than Summer Garden and more fair
It was. We never knew that soon we'd only
Look backward in complete despair.

January 1917

WE CAN'T SEEM TO SAY OUR GOODBYE

We can't seem to say our goodbye—
And shoulder to shoulder we walk.
Already it's dark in the sky,
You are pensive, and I don't talk.

Let's enter a church and we'll see
A christening, a wedding, a wake.
Not exchanging a glance, we'll leave. . .
Is it all for us both a mistake?

Or we'll sit in the trampled snow
By the graves, and softly we'll sigh,
As you draw with a stick to show
The place where we'll always reside.

1917

PRAYER

Give me ages of bitterness wild,
Suffocation, insomnia, rage,
Take away both my lover and child,
And the songs that I sing for my age—
This I pray as I suffer Your passion,
After so many agonized days,
That the tempest that hangs over Russia
Might become a bright nimbus of rays.

May 1915
Day of the Holy Ghost
St. Petersburg

SUCH DAYS AS THESE OCCUR
BEFORE THE SPRING

Such days as these occur before the spring:
Beneath the heavy snow the meadows rest,
The dessicated trees in pleasure sing,
And balmy winds grow tender-soft and deft.
Your body marvels at its lack of weight,
You hardly recognize the house and view;
And songs you found so tedious of late,
You sing with deep emotion, as if new.

Spring 1915
Slepnyovo

ALL GOLD AND WIDE IS EVENING'S GLOW

All gold and wide is evening's glow,
As April's tender chill is cast.
You should have come some years ago,
But I am glad you're here at last.

Come close and sit beside me here,
And with a joyful eye take note
Of this blue book from yesteryear—
With all the girlish verse I wrote.

Forgive me that I lived in pain,
That in the sun my joys were few.
Forgive as well that I in vain
Mistook so many men for you.

Spring 1915
Tsarskoye Selo

HE NEVER MOCKED, DID NOT EXTOL

He never mocked, did not extol,
As have my friends and foes,
He only left his mortal soul
And told me: guard it close.

And now one worry haunts my mind:
If he should die today,
God's Angel then will come to find
And take his soul away.

How then can I conceal it, though?
How keep from God my prize?
This soul that sobs and warbles so
Should be in Paradise.

July 1915

IT'S A MONDAY. THE TWENTY-FIRST. NIGHT

It's a Monday. The twenty-first. Night.
All the shapes of the city are blurred.
Oh, some idler invented the lie
That there's something called love on this earth.

And from boredom or lazy complacence,
All believed, and they wait evermore
For the trysts, and they dread separation,
And they sing of the one they adore.

But some others will learn the great secret,
And the knowledge will render them still. . .
I myself didn't knowingly seek it
And it seems ever since have been ill.

1917
Petersburg

I KNOW THAT YOU ARE MY REWARD

I know that you are my reward
For years of trouble and of blight,
For never giving all my heart
To earthly pleasure and delight,
For never saying to a friend:
"I love you more than all my cares."
Since I forgave them in the end,
You'll be the angel of my prayers.

1916

AND SO IT SEEMS—A HUMAN SOUND

And so it seems—a human sound
Is never sounded here,
The stone-age wind is all that pounds
Against the backyard pier.
It seems to me that I alone
Beneath this sky survive—
Since I was she who early chose
To drink the deadly wine.

Summer 1917
Slepnyovo

I WAS BORN NEITHER EARLY NOR LATE

I was born neither early nor late,
At a time that was blest and unique,
But the Lord didn't grant me the fate
Of a heart that would live undeceived.

This is why in my room I sit grieving,
This is why all the lovers I've known,
Like the sorrowful birds of the evening,
Sing a love that has never been shown.

1913

OH, THERE ARE WORDS ONE CAN'T REPEAT

Oh, there are words—one can't repeat,
And one who speaks them—spends too much.
The only things we can't deplete
Are Heaven's blue and Mercy's touch.

Winter 1916
Sevastopol

From *Plantain*

BOTH MY WINDOW SHADES ARE OPEN

Both my window shades are open,
You can look right in my room;
I take pleasure now in knowing,
You can't bear to leave too soon.
You may call me a poor sinner,
You may mock me out of spite:
I'm the cause of your not sleeping,
I'm your anguish in the night.

1916

SUDDEN SILENCE FILLS MY QUARTERS

Sudden silence fills my quarters,
Now the poppy sheds its bloom,
I am deep in drowsy waters
And have met an early gloom.

All the gates are tightly barred,
Night is black, the winds are few.
Where is laughter, where regard,
Where, my tender groom, are you?

I have lost the secret circlet,
I have waited many days,
Like a captive bird my verses
Are as silent as the grave.

July 1917
Slepnyovo

WHY CONSTANTLY COME AND KEEP MOANING *(a fragment)*[25]

Why constantly come and keep moaning
Beneath my high window all day?
You know you won't drown in the ocean,
And you'll always be safe in the fray.

Neither ocean nor battle is dreadful
For one who has forfeited grace.
Which is why you've asked me to mention
Your name every time when I pray.

Summer 1917
Slepnyovo

AND INTO A SECRETIVE FRIENDSHIP

And into a secretive friendship
With one who has dark, eagle eyes,
As into a late-summer garden,
I entered on steps that were light.
Last roses were blooming around me,
And a crystalline moon was adrift
In the billowing gray of the clouds. . .

Summer 1917
St. Petersburg

WHEN HE RECEIVES BELATED WORD

When he receives belated word
Of my most bitter death,
He will not grow more sad or grave,
But, turning pale, he'll catch his breath.
And he'll recall the Neva's shore,
A raging blizzard and its strife,
And then recall how once he swore
To guard his eastern lady's life.

1917

WHEN PEOPLE PONDERED SUICIDE

When people pondered suicide
Awaiting German guests in dread;
When Russia's Church had lost her pride
And Byzantine stern spirit fled;

And when the Neva's stately Queen,[26]
Forgetting history's gloried text,
Turned drunken slut and roamed the street,
Not knowing who would have her next—

I heard a distant voice command:
"Come here!" Then soothingly it said:
"Depart your sorry, sinful land,
Leave Russia as one leaves the dead.

I'll rid your heart of this black shame
And wash the blood from hands and feet;
I'll blanket with another name
The pain of insult and defeat."

But calmly and with cold disdain
I placed my hands upon my ears,
Lest these unworthy words profane
My mournful spirit and my tears.

1917

ONCE I ASKED A CUCKOO GAILY

Once I asked a cuckoo gaily,
Would I live for many days. . .
Pine and fir were gently swaying,
On the grass fell yellow rays,
But no sound from grove or freshet. . .
I am leaving now,
As the cooling breeze caresses
My still burning brow.

1 June 1919
Tsarskoye Selo

IN EACH FULL DAY RESIDES

In each full day resides
A dark and anxious hour.
Not opening my eyes,
I talk to grief aloud;
It only beats, like blood,
Or like the breath of heat,
Like happy, sated love,
Malicious in its greed.

1917

ALL EARTHLY FAME IS LIKE SMOKE

All earthly fame is like smoke,
It isn't the thing I sought.
To all the lovers I've known
Great joy and delight I brought.
And one even now survives,
In love with his lady fair;
Another has turned to bronze
And stands in a snowlit square.

Winter 1914

AND HERE AM I, LEFT ALL ALONE

And here am I, left all alone
To count each empty day.
O friends who left me on my own,
O swans who flew away!

I cannot summon you with song
Or bring you back with tears,
But all the solemn evening long
I'll keep you in my prayers.

For one of you death's arrow came,
And you, anointed, fell;
The other, kissing me, became
A raven black as hell.

But as it happens: once a year,
When ice begins to thaw,
In Catherine's garden I appear,
Where sacred waters fall. . .[27]

And hear the splash of spreading wings
Upon the glacial blue.
I do not know who let the wind
Inside the dungeon tomb.

1917

WHY IS THIS AGE MORE BLEAK

Why is this age more bleak than those that came before?
That in its haze of sorrow and of woe
It lightly touched the blackest sore,
But could not make it whole.

The earthly sun still gleams upon the western shores,
And in its glowing rays the roofs of cities shine,
While here a pallid shade with crosses marks the doors
And calls the ravens round, and ravens fill the skies.

Winter 1919

THERE'S NO ONE NOW TO HEAR A SONG

There's no one now to hear a song.
The days foretold have come about.
My final song, our world has gone,
Don't break my heart; do not resound.

Not long ago, a swallow free,
You made your flight in early morn,
But now a beggar you shall be,
To knock in vain at strangers' doors.

1917

ALONG THE HARD CRUST OF THE SNOW

Along the hard crust of the snow,
Surrounded by silence complete,
We both of us quietly go
To your secret white house of retreat.
And sweeter than all the songs sung
Is having this dream come alive,
The swaying of branches we've rung—
Your spurs and their delicate chime.

January 1917

AT NIGHT

The moon is scarce alive above the yard,
Half hidden in the cloud-bescattered sky,
And by the palace gates the sullen guard
Surveys the tower clock with angry eye.

The faithless wife is on her way back home,
Her face is darkly pensive and severe,
And, in a dream's embrace, the faithful wife
Is burning in the grip of endless fear.

But what are they to me? A week ago
I took a breath and told the world goodbye—
It stifled me—and to the park I stole
To look at stars and make my lyre sigh.

Autumn 1918
Moscow

THE RIVER FLOWS, UNHURRIED

The river flows, unhurried, through the grain,
A many-windowed house upon a rise.
We live the way they did in Catherine's reign:
We offer prayers and wait for harvest time.
A caller, having borne two days of parting,
Comes riding through the golden fields of rye,
He kisses granny's hand inside the parlor
And on the curving stair my lips and eyes.

Summer 1917
Slepnyovo

A STRING OF BEADS AROUND THE THROAT

A string of beads around the throat
The hands inside a muff I hide.
These eyes look vacantly about
And will not ever after cry.

Against the lilac-colored crepe
The face looks even paler now,
The forelock lies so flat and straight
It almost reaches to the brow.

And how unlike unfettered flight
This halting step with which I go,
As if a raft were underfoot
And not the parquet squares I know.

Pale lips just slightly held apart,
Irregular and labored breathing,
And trembling up against my heart
The blossoms of an unheld meeting.

1913

THE WHOLE DAY LONG, WITH FEARFUL CRIES

The whole day long, with fearful cries,
The crowd in anguished grieving quakes,
Across the creek, at funeral rites,
Malicious skulls with laughter shake.
And this is why I sang as well,
They tore my heart to shreds,
As, after shelling, stillness fell,
And Death patrolled the dead.

Summer 1917

I SHOULD DREAM OF YOU FAR LESS OFTEN

I should dream of you far less often,
For we meet many times in the light,
But you seem so much sadder and softer
Only then, in the still of the night.
How much sweeter than praises of angels
Are the dear lying words that you say. . .
Oh, in dreams you don't ever misname me,
Or sigh as you do in the day.

1914

From *Anno Domini MCMXXI*

PROPHECY

Oh, I too have beheld the gold crown. . .
Do not seek such a crown for yourself!
It was stolen, you see, and not found,
And it wouldn't become you too well.
Like a briarthorn's tight twisted bough,
It would glitter, my crown, upon you;
Never mind that your delicate brow
It would freshen with roseate dew.

8 May 1922 [28]

HE SAID I HAVE NO RIVALS

He said I have no rivals, not a one.
I'm not an earthly woman in his eyes,
But rather the consoling winter sun,
The savage song his native country cries.

Yet when I die, he will not madly cry:
"Rise up again!"—nor will he grieve for long,
But he will learn, the flesh cannot survive
Without the sun, the soul without a song.
But what of now?

1921

DO NOT TORMENT YOUR HEART

Do not torment your heart with earth's delights,
Do not become attached to home or wife,
Deprive your tender infant of his bread
To give it to a stranger's use instead.
And be the humblest servant of another,
Of him who was your most relentless foe,
And call the forest beast your only brother,
And never ask the Lord to ease your woe.

December 1921
Petersburg

NO KIN AM I TO THOSE WHO LEFT

No kin am I to those who left
Their land to slaughter from its foes.
Their coarse enticements find me deaf,
No songs for them do I compose.

But pity banished souls, I pray,
Like convicts or the deathly ill.
Dark is the traveler's homeless way,
The stranger's bread a bitter pill.

But here in conflagration's fumes,
In sacrifice of youth's remains,
We have not faltered or refused
A single blow as dealt by fate.

We know that when accounts are paid,
Each action will be justified. . .
But on this earth no people stayed
More simply proud, or drier-eyed.

July 1922
Petersburg

EACH MORNING THE FROST IS A GLAZE

Each morning the frost is a glaze,
It rustles and crackles, it's fine;
The bush in a blinding white blaze
Is heavy with roses of ice;
And there on the great snowy stage
The traces of skis are a sign,
That once in a long-ago age
We traveled this way, you and I.

1922

WE WILL NOT MEET

We will not meet. We stand opposed.
What insolence to call me now
To where my brother, bloodied, rose,
An angel's crown upon his brow.

And neither your entreating eyes,
Nor any savage vow you swore,
Nor yet the shiver of those sighs
From that ecstatic love I bore
    Will now seduce. . .

June 1921

TERROR, PICKING AT THINGS IN THE DARK

Terror, picking at things in the dark,
Leads the moonbeam to an ax.
Behind the wall a sinister knock—
Is it rats, a ghost, a thief perhaps?

In the muggy kitchen water drips,
Keeping count with the creaking boards.
Someone's there! . . a shiny black beard
Flashes past the window pane,—

And freezes. How evil and stealthy he is,
Hiding the matches, blowing the candles out.
Oh, better the gleaming of barrels,
Of rifles leveled at my breast.

Better the grassy square—
Mounting the raw wooden planks;
Under the cheers and moans
To empty my body of blood.

I press the smooth cross to my heart:
Restore, O God, peace to my soul!
Corruption's smell, swooningly sweet,
Rises from chilly damp sheets.

27-28 August 1921 [29]
Tsarskoye Selo

Other Poems

THE MUSE

When I await her coming in the night,
It seems that life is hanging by a thread.
But what is honor, youth, or freedom's right
Compared to her, who bears a flute instead?

Then she appeared. And casting off her mantle,
Attentively she looked me in the eye.
I asked her: "Was it you who read to Dante
Inferno's pages? And she answered: "I."

1924

HERE PUSHKIN'S YEARS OF BANISHMENT COMMENCED

Here Pushkin's years of banishment commenced
And Lermontov from banishment was freed.
Here mountain herbs convey their subtle scents,
And only once was I allowed to see,
Beside the lake, amid the shaded forest,
In that cruel time when twilight mounts the skies,
The radiance that haunts the thirsting eyes
Of that immortal lover of Tamara.[30]

1927
Kislovodsk

COUPLET

From others all praises are haze,
From you even censure is praise.

1931

THE FINAL TOAST

I drink to my forsaken home,
To all the woes I knew,
I drink to lovers, each alone,
And drink, my friend, to you,—
To faithless lips that told me lies,
To frigid deathly eyes,
To all the cruelty life entailed,
And to the God that failed.

1934

SENTENCE[31]

Upon my living breathing breast
The stony word abruptly fell.
No matter, though—for I was set
And now will deal with this as well.

I have so much to do today:
I need to stifle memory's ken,
I need my soul to burn away,
I need to learn to live again,—

If not... The rustling summer heat
Outside my door is on carouse.
I sensed long since that I would meet
This sunlit day, this vacant house.

June 22, 1939
Fountain House

CRUCIFIXION

Mary Magdalene wept in despair,
A disciple was turning to stone;
Not a soul dared to glance over there,
Where the Mother stood silent, alone.

1939

CLEOPATRA

The palaces of Alexandria
Were covered with a sweet shade.
   —Pushkin[32]

She's kissed the dead lips of her Antony's corpse,
Has shed on her knees before Caesar hot tears. . .
Her servants have fled. The victorious horns
Of Rome are resounding, and darkness appears.

And in came the last whom her beauty enslaved,
Most stately and tall, and he blushed as he swore:
"He'll send you before him in triumph, a slave."
But calm as a swan's was her neck as before.

Tomorrow they'll shackle her children in chains.
So little to do. . . but to jest with this man. . .
And then the black snake, as a parting to pain,
To place on her breast with dispassionate hand.

17 February 1940

BUT I AM WARNING YOU

But I am warning you that now
I'm living for the final time.
Not as a bird or maple bough,
Not as a belfry's distant chime,
Not as a star or rustling reed,
Not as a spring-fed waterfall—
Will I now trouble people's peace
Or ever visit others' dreams
With my inconsolable call.

1940

STANZAS

A Streltsy moon above. The Moscow River. Night.[33]
And Passion Week proceeds like Stations of the Cross.
I see a dreadful dream. Can all be truly lost?
Can no one, no one, no one help me in my plight?

Czar Peter spake the truth: "No life in Kremlin walls."—
Inside still teem the germs of ancient bloodied fate:
Czar Boris with his dread, the Ivans with their hate,
The false Pretender's pride—while still the people calls.

April 1940
Moscow

WHENEVER SOMEONE DIES

Whenever someone dies,
His portraits seem to change:
A difference in the eyes,
The smiling lips so strange.
I noticed this one night
At some poor poet's rite,
And since that time I've checked—
And found that I'm correct.

1940

COURAGE

What hangs in the balance is clear,
And what we must all now endure;
The moment for courage is here,
And courage will keep us secure.
No bullet will cause us to weep,
Lost homes are not bitter to bear;
And we will preserve you, our Speech,
O Great Russian Word in our care!
For children unborn you shall be
Unsullied and living and free
    Forever!

1942

PUSHKIN

Who knows what glory's crown implies!
What price he paid to claim that prize,
The right or grace or happy chance
To laugh with wisdom's cunning eyes,
Keep silent with a secret glance,
And mark both dancer and the dance?[34]

1943

OURS IS AN ANCIENT, SACRED TRADE

Ours is an ancient, sacred trade.
Thousands of years it's still survived. . .
Light for a lightless world it made;
And not one poet yet has cried
That age and wisdom only lied;
And maybe death itself has died.

1944

FROM AN AIRPLANE

A hundred versts, a hundred miles,
A hundred kilométers—
There lay the salt, there grasses sighed,
And darkled groves of cedars.
It seemed the first and only time,
I'd seen my homeland whole.
I knew that all I saw was mine—
My body and my soul.

May 1944

TEACHER

In memory of Innokenty Annensky[35]

And he, whom I consider teacher,
Has vanished and has left no trace.
He drank the deadly nightshade down,
Awaiting fame that never came.
He was the portent and precursor,
Who pitied all, inhaled their stillness—
And choked to death. . .

1945

LIBERATION

Clean wind is rocking the firs,
Clean snow is embracing the fields.
The enemy's tread is unheard,
My land to serenity yields.

February 1945

HE'S RIGHT—ONCE MORE THE LAMP[36]

He's right—once more the lamp, the druggist's store,
The Neva, silence, granite banks. . .
And there he stands, this man, once more,
A monument to mark the age—
And when he bade the Pushkin House
Farewell and raised his hand to wave,
He wore a mortal weariness,
A dusky cloak of undue peace.

1946

EPIGRAM

Could Beatrice, as Dante did, create,
Or Laura sing of love and passion's heat?
I've taught our women how to speak of late,
But, Lord, I ask you. . . how to make them cease!

1958

THE DEATH OF THE POET

Echo will answer me like a bird.
  —*Boris Pasternak*

A voice is stilled that will not sound again,
For he who spoke with groves has quit our band.
He's turned into the life-bestowing grain
Or all the gentle showers that he sang.
And all the flowers that this world can hold
To meet this death have blossomed into birth.
But suddenly the globe is hushed and cold—
This planet with the humble name. . . of Earth.

1 June 1960
Botkinsky Hospital
Moscow

THE DEATH OF SOPHOCLES

And then the Czar knew well,
That Sophocles had died.
  —A legend

To Sophocles's house an eagle flew that night,
And from the garden tolled cicadas' mournful calls,
While his immortal soul right then was taking flight
And passed the hostile host that stormed his city's walls.
And that was when the Czar beheld a dreadful dream:
Grim Dionysus spoke and bade him halt the fight,
That tumult not disturb the sacramental scene,
And all the Athens men might praise the poet's light.

1961

ALEXANDER AT THEBES

No doubt the youthful king was dread and cold
When he pronounced destruction on the town.
The agèd captain shuddered to behold
That ancient haughty city of renown.

Go torch it all! And so the king made note
Of towers, gates, and temples—to be razed,
But then he mused and, brightening, he spoke:
"Just look you that the poet's house be saved."

October 1961
The Hospital in the Harbor
Leningrad

Poem Index

POEM INDEX

From *Plantain*

From *Anno Domini MCMXXI*

Notes and Credits

ENDNOTES

[1] Numbers in parentheses refer to the page numbers of cited poems in this collection.

[2] Anna Akhmatova, *Rekviem: v piati knigakh*, R. D. Timenchik and K. M. Polivanov, eds. (Moscow: Izdatel'stvo MPI, 1989), 302. The "Yezhov Terror" refers to the state-sponsored mass repressions of the late 1930s under chief of secret police N. I. Yezhov. The translation is mine.

[3] Technically speaking, the meter of this poem is a dol'nik—in which strongly stressed syllables are separated by either one or two unstressed syllables. Yet it tends markedly towards the anapest—in which two unstressed syllables always lie between the stressed ones.

[4] Compare, for instance, the tone and song-like regularity of Dickenson:

I hide myself within my flower,
That wearing on your breast,
You, unsuspecting, wear me too—
And angels know the rest.

I hide myself within my flower,
That, fading from your vase,
You, unsuspecting, feel for me
Almost a loneliness.

[5] Marina Tsvetaeva (1892-1941), Akhmatova's close contemporary, must be mentioned as the other leading force in this transformation of the place of women in Russia's literary life. Earlier women poets who number among Akhmatova's predecessors are Karolina Pavlova (1807-1893) and Zinaida Gippius (1869-1945). Very significant, in their own unique ways, the reputations of these poets in their own time and subsequently are of an entirely different magnitude than those of Akhmatova and Tsvetaeva, whose careers reordered the literary landscape to such an extent that celebrated Russian women writers ceased being out of the ordinary.

[6] Osip Mandel'shtam, "Pis'mo o russkoi poezii," *Sobranie sochinenii v cheterekh tomakh*, 4 vols. (Moscow: Art-biznes-tsentr, 1993), ii.

236-40, cit. on 239. The translation is mine. Nikolai S. Leskov (1831-1895) is a noted nineteenth-century author of somewhat lesser reputation in the West than the other undisputed "greats" mentioned here by Mandelstam.

[7] In a study published the same year as Mandelstam's remark, the Russian formalist critic Boris Eikhenbaum devoted considerable energy to consideration of the novelistic qualities of Akhmatova's works, suggesting that the poems should be read in aggregate as "fragments of a mosaic, which knit together and form something akin to a large novel." Boris Eikhenbaum, *Anna Akhmatova* (Paris: Lev, 1985), 121. The translation is mine.

[8] Joseph Brodsky, "The Keening Muse," in his: *Less Than One: Selected Essays* (New York: Farrar Straus Giroux, 1986), 36.

[9] Andrew Wachtel and Ilya Vinitsky, *A Cultural History of Russian Literature* (Cambridge: Polity Press, 2009), 178.

[10] Prior to the revolution of 1917, Russian dates were recorded according to the Julian calendar, by which Akhmatova was born on June 11. All dates in this introduction have been adjusted to the modern Gregorian calendar.

[11] Nikolai A. Nekrasov (1821-1878) is an important Russian poet known for his progressive sentiments and civic themes.

[12] Brodsky, "The Keening Muse," 35.

[13] Cited in: Roberta Reeder, "Mirrors and Masks: The Life and Poetic Works of Anna Akhmatova" in: Roberta Reeder, ed., *The Complete Poems of Anna Akhmatova*, Judith Hemschemeyer, trans. (Somerville, Mass.: Zephyr Press, 1990), 93.

[14] From a 1922 newspaper article in Molodaia gvardiia by S.A. Rodov, a minor poet and member of the Russian Association of Proletarian Writers. Reprinted in: Akhmatova, *Rekviem: v piati knigakh*, 53. The translation in mine.

[15] "Iz sokrashchennoi i obobshchennoi stenogrammy dokladov t. Zhdanova na sobranii partiinogo aktiva i na sobranii pisatelei v Leningrade," in: Akhmatova, *Rekviem: v piati knigakh*, 237. The translation is mine.

[16] "Tsarskoye Selo" is the fashionable suburb of St. Petersburg where Akhmatova spent her childhood. The town's name may be translated literally as "Tsar's Village," and reflects the location there of the Imperial summer residence.

[17] The "swarthy youth," of the poem is A. S. Pushkin (1799-1837), Russia's national poet, who attended the Lycée in Tsarskoye Selo. The epithet "swarthy" references Pushkin's Abyssinian or "African" (in the poet's words) forbear, a protégé of Peter the Great. The reference in the last line is to the French neoclassical poet, Évariste Desiré de Forges, vicomte de Parny (1753-1814), who influenced Pushkin.

[18] "White nights" is the term used in northern Russia to refer to summer evenings when the sun sets only for a few hours and full darkness never arrives.

[19] The title of an early draft of the poem was "In the Stray Dog," identifying the scene described here as the avant-garde artistic and literary cabaret of that name in St. Petersburg.

[20] St. Petersburg is situated on the mouths of the Neva River, the periodic flooding of which became a subject of literary representation in Pushkin's important poem "The Bronze Horseman." "Paul's fortress" refers to another St. Petersburg landmark, the Mikhailovskii Fortress, which was the residence of Emperor Paul I (1796-1801).

[21] These two poems reference St. Isaac's Cathedral, the Galernyi Arch and the monument to Peter the Great immortalized in Pushkin's important poem "The Bronze Horseman." These landmarks all stand on or around Senate Square in St. Petersburg.

[22] Alexander Blok (1880-1921) was a leading Symbolist poet. Akhmatova visited him on December 15, 1913. This poem was in response to a poem that Blok dedicated to Akhmatova. Both poems were initially published together in the journal *Love for Three Oranges*, for which Blok served as poetry editor.

[23] Nikolai V. Nedobrovo (1882-1919), a friend of Akhmatova, was a poet and critic.

[24] Vasily A. Komarovsky (1881-1914), was a poet whom Akhmatova admired. This poem is evidently a reply to Komarovsky's poem

"To Anna Akhmatova," which was published posthumously in 1914.

[25] These are the final two stanzas of the poem "You are a renegade..."

[26] The "Neva's stately queen" refers to St Petersburg, which is situated on the mouths of the river Neva.

[27] "Catherine's garden" refers to the Imperial parks in Tsarskoe Selo.

[28] The poem was composed on the anniversary of Akhmatova's wedding to Nikolai Gumilev.

[29] Akhmatova's first husband, Nikolai Gumilev, was executed on August 25, 1921.

[30] Kislovodsk, a spa town in the Caucasus mountains in southern Russia, was a location visited by Russia's two greatest Romantic poets, Pushkin and M. Iu Lermontov (1814-1841), during periods of political exile imposed on them for subversive poetic compositions. Lermontov died in a duel that took place in the region. "Tamara's lover" is a reference to the title character of one of Lermontov's best-known poems, "The Demon."

[31] This poem and the next form parts of Akhmatova's celebrated cycle of poems treating the Stalinist Terror, *Requiem*. The date of this poem's composition is the day Akhmatova's son Lev Gumilev was sentenced to a term in prison camp.

[32] The epigraph is derived from Pushkin's poem "Cleopatra."

[33] "Streltsy" refers to the special Muscovite military class that was a source of opposition to Peter the Great early in his reign. Following an attempted revolt against the young tsar in 1698, a large number of Streltsy were publicly executed, their regiments were disbanded and their privileges abolished.

[34] Translator's note: I have taken liberties with this final line, which in the Russian contains an untranslatable play on words that refers to Pushkin's description in *Eugene Onegin* of a ballerina's dancing feet.

[35] Innokenty F. Annensky (1855-1909) was a Symbolist poet whose works influenced Akhmatova in her earliest period.

[36] This poem is in belated reply to a well-known poem by Blok, offered here in a new translation by James Falen:

Night. . . street. . . a lamp. . .a druggist's store,
A dim and senseless light about.
Oh, one could live for decades more—
With nothing changed. With no way out.

You'll die. . . and once again begin,
And all will happen as before:
The night, the channel's icy glint,
The street, the lamp, the druggist's store.

1912

All poems selected and translated by James E. Falen
Indroductory essay "Anna Akhmatova: Lyricism and Endurance"
by Kevin M. F. Platt

First published in softcover in the United States of America by
Whale & Star, Delray Beach, Florida
info@whaleandstar.com, www.whaleandstar.com

Design Concept: The people of Whale & Star
Lead Publication Coordinator: Jillian Taylor, Catherine Wallack
Copy: Tessa Blumenberg, Jillian Taylor
Editor: Kevin M. F. Platt
Translator: James E. Falen

Cover: Amedeo Modigliani, *Kneeling Caryatid,* reproduced courtesy
of Richard Nathanson, London

Distributed exclusively by University of Nebraska Press
1111 Lincoln Mall
Lincoln, Nebraska 68588-0630
www.nebraskapress.unl.edu
Tel: 800/755 1105
Fax: 800/526 2617

Library of Congress Control Number: 2009933368

ISBN: 978-0-9799752-3-3